conversations in parked cars

conversations in parked cars

grace kuhn

ISBN-13: 979-8-218-65091-9

Library of Congress Control Number: 2025906297

PRINTED IN THE UNITED STATES OF AMERICA

to all our broken pieces
may we heal them
bit by bit, word by word

forward

I've always said that I can only write poems when I feel strong emotions. Euphoric highs. Miserable lows. When I feel like life can't get any better and when I feel broken past the point of repair. Hurt, betrayal, heartbreak, anxiety, and grief. Happiness, compassion, freedom, joy, and connection. Falling in love and falling apart. I reach for poetry when I can't find my middle ground, when there's a weight on my chest I need to relieve, when I need to flesh out my thoughts in order to make sense of and learn from my experiences. I find that when I'm not writing it's usually because I don't want to be honest with myself, when I'm afraid of the pages and their potent truth serum. This is the exact reason why I went on a long hiatus from writing poetry recently.

It was in those months that so many thoughts built up inside my head, thoughts I feared to write down because that would make them real. After a late night conversation with my friends at the start of our spring semester, something inside of me cracked open and every last word came flooding out. It felt as if I had been stuck, running myself to the point of exhaustion on a treadmill leading me nowhere. I didn't know it yet, but that moment shaped the person I was becoming, the newest and oldest version of me. A version my mom likes to refer to as Grace 2.0.

From there forward, my life underwent many changes. At times it was overwhelming, but it was also liberating. For the first time in my life, I put myself first and gave myself the permission to be okay with not having everything figured out. I turned to poetry to make sense of it all and realized I hadn't written like that in months. I felt a slight tug then that there was meaning in the timing.

The idea for this book came about three years ago when I faced what I thought just might be the worst heartbreak of my life. I was eighteen and can safely say now that that girl had no idea what real love or real heartbreak was, but oh did she feel everything to the fullest extent. She compiled all of the poems she had ever written into a Google Doc entitled *conversations in parked cars*. This document became her safe haven, her constant, her coping mechanism. For the next three years, she would continue to write and empty every broken piece of her into this document, which grew longer and longer by the week. She thought she would never release it. It was too personal, and besides, who reads poetry anyway?

This is why I'm a person who believes in timing. I believe the universe has a way of putting people and opportunities in our paths and a way of preventing us from things we're not meant for or not ready for yet. I wasn't ready at fifteen or at eighteen. There was still so much to experience, so much to learn, so much to write. It was all leading up to now.

My parents always told me that as much as college was going to teach me about academics, it would teach me even more about life. I rolled my eyes, but they couldn't have been more right. I'm starting to realize parents usually are when it comes to this stuff. Because college redefined my relationship with myself. It broke me down, but also healed me in places I didn't know were still hurting. These past two and a half years have brought me to this new yet old version of myself that made me realize people pleasing would get me nowhere and that the hardest decisions usually lead to the most fulfilling outcomes. It taught me that imperfections and wrong decisions give you stories, and stories make life remarkable. It taught me that love must first come from yourself, and there's nothing like a hug from your mom and dad and the circle of friends you felt you were meant to find. It taught me to trust my gut instead of the worries spinning in my head. It taught me that the pieces of me that felt broken were the same pieces that fueled my creativity. It taught me that my words held power, even if they only ever meant something to me.

My life changed because I finally decided to take control of it. No one, not even the anxious tendencies of my mind, would be allowed to hold the reins any longer.

Stepping into those realizations and weeks of writing with fervent passion, I felt called to do this. This was the moment, *my* moment.

This book is a piece of my soul. There is no exaggeration in that sentence. These are words I've held onto for the last six years of my life, tucked into notebooks in desk drawers or locked files on my laptop. Words I've never let even those closest to me read. This is the place all of my thoughts and ideas take residence in, find solace in. I mean it to the fullest extent when I say these are words I never intended for anyone to read.

To step into this new phase, I felt the need to let these words go. Because by setting them free, I'm also setting myself free.

This is a collection of poems that spans six years, from ages fifteen to twenty-one. It's a montage of real experiences and fictional stories, honest and raw emotions. Good, bad, ugly, and beautiful all tied up in the lopsided bow we call young adulthood. It's messy, imperfect, and chaotic, but I think that's what makes it magical.

For me, it's been such a unique experience to look back on all these poems and realize I accidentally created a scrapbook of my teenage years. I can read a poem and know exactly who I was and how I felt at the time. Sometimes I cringe. Sometimes I smile. Most of all I look back in awe at the transformation.

So, this is for the little girl who wrote stories on construction paper. The girl who was always drawn to words in a way most couldn't understand. For the eleven year old who found that writing was the only way to feel at peace with the grief from losing those she loved. For the fifteen year old who was too scared to put herself out there. The girl who felt like she experienced emotions too deeply in a world that was always pushing you to just keep moving, to get on the next train. And for the girl writing this forward in a parked car on a Friday afternoon. Because it always starts and ends in the same place for me.

With *conversations in parked cars.*

conversations in parked cars

nothing
good
comes
from
conversations
in
parked cars

i was here

i feel
like my voice
is so small
as if my words
bounce out of my mouth
and ricochet
right back in
never reaching
the ears of others
sometimes
i feel like i talk and talk
but no one listens
no one hears
i don't wonder why
because my words
must be so
insignificant
in a world full of people
with so much to say
sometimes
i go silent
let my thoughts gather up
in my mind
and at the tip of my tongue
locked inside
by some invisible cage
the world doesn't seem to notice
my silent treatments
so once I feel too full
of all my thoughts
i let them pour
out of my mouth
like black coffee
but they are lost

behind the screams of others
their thoughts
stronger
more powerful
than mine
because i am small
and my voice is quiet
so instead
i fill these blank pages
with the words i feel
in my heart
and the thoughts that consume my mind
pages and pages of words
that mean nothing
or maybe everything
words other people may never understand
but i start to find comfort in that
because i know that with each page
i write
i am making my mark on the world
even if it is not heard
or seen just yet
i know that one day my words
will be all that is left of me
a million ways of saying
i was here

shallow water

i just keep holding on to
nothing
the shallow waters
of your ocean blue eyes
i dove head first
and maybe it's my fault
for falling too hard
for expecting you to follow through
on all your promises
if that's the reason we fell apart
then i guess
i'm the one to blame
for the way every bone in my body aches
when i think about you
which
if you were wondering
is all the time
they say the best revenge
is doing okay
but how can i even pretend to be doing
alright
when i lay awake
all night just thinking about you
and us
even though there isn't even an us
anymore
and maybe
there never really was

his

i don't remember who i am anymore
i am not sure where along the lines i lost myself
but i did
at those parties
you used to bring me to
you would introduce me as
your girlfriend
those people all knew me
as *his girlfriend*
that title became more meaningful
than my own name
i was yours
was
i wish i could say *am*
but i'm not yours anymore
so who am i?
just a girl
who walks through the streets of this town
with her head down
because everytime
she looks up
all she sees
are the memories
playing out like film scenes
ghosts
of people who used to be
maybe all i am
is the shell of the girl
who used to be yours
with no real
identity
anymore
because
i gave up all the parts that made me

who i was
to be yours
so if i am no longer me
and i am no longer yours
then who am i?

i am from

i am from coffee cups
from mizuno running shoes and fishing poles
i am from the backyard fire pit with adirondack chairs
starry skies and the smell of smoke
surrounded by family and friends
who are more like chosen family
i am from oak trees and pink hydrangeas
that grow in memory of my grandmother who died too soon
i'm from sunday football and christmas cookie day
road races and parade days in march
from freckles and blue eyes
from geraldine and john joseph
i'm from vineyard trips and eye rolls
from *you can't run without your pepper spray*
and *good night i love you see you in the morning sweet dreams*
i'm from *i can't smile without you* and *amazing grace*
dave matthews and pearl jam
cornelia street and oregon street
from cross necklaces and love
i'm from westfield and ireland
pierogies and pecan tassies
from my grandfather's air force plane crash
from my mother and father slow dancing to yellow by coldplay
the boxes of my grandmother's pictures
that span over decades in rubbermaid boxes
capturing all of the good times
i am from the moments a phone could not catch
the memories that won't grow old with time

habitual

your pinky
brushed up against mine
ever so slightly
it could have been an accident
or at least
that's what i told myself in those few seconds
as your hand moved away
but slowly
your fingers reached out
intertwining with mine
it was the habitual nature
of it
that caught me off guard
filled with the same ease and comfort
of taking your first sip of coffee
in the morning

happy ever after

i thought
we could rewrite
the ending of our story
thought we could tear
out the last few chapters
and replace them
little did i know
it didn't matter
how many words i wrote
or how pretty you tried to make them sound
or how many details i wish i could change
we could write
an entirely
different
story
and it would still
end
the same
way

my garage

you shook my dad's hand
impressed my mom
that day
followed me home as the rain started
and when i told you i was tired
you offered to make me a coffee
while i got ready for the next party
you pulled me close
in the kitchen
arms wrapped tight around me
and asked
did you have a fun day?
my friends were texting
and we were late
so i led you into the garage
but you stopped
and pulled me to your chest
i could feel your heart throbbing
so hard and fast
it was as if i were listening
through a stethoscope
i could feel
your eyes hovering over me
but i was too nervous
to look up
you let go
and i started to walk away
wait
you said
there's one more thing i want to do
i turned back
and then you kissed me
for the first time
and it didn't matter

that we were in the middle of my
not-so-romantic
garage
or that we were in a rush
it was you and me
lost in a moment i had been waiting for
and dreaming of
for months
i felt like i had you
for the first time
three days later
you were gone
and i was left wondering
how someone
could change their mind
so
damn
fast

every great love story

peter
lost wendy
and rose
lost jack
romeo
lost juliet
and i
lost you
i guess
every great
love
story
must come
to an
end
i just
didn't think
ours would
end
so
soon

love is in the air

to all the people
who say
love
is in the air -
exactly what air
are you
breathing?
and where
can i
find it?

thunder storm

you
are the
rain
an evening
thunder
storm
beautiful
to watch from the window
tragic
to get caught up in

evicted

he plucks the strings of his guitar
hoping his sentimental words can bring her back
she listens at her window, present, but not at all
her eyes cold, color they lack
his face, a shadow of comfort
his eyes, holes of despair
her hands hold his heart, in total control
destroy it? she wouldn't dare
his heart wanders around without her
it doesn't have a home
she paces around her bedroom floor
as he sings with oblivious hope
how will she tell him there's someone new
and she is his no more?

scrapbook

heaven is a scrapbook of lives
with moments painted black and white
and memories singing in color

pictures of the one that got away
pictures of the good old days
pictures of nights you thought would never end
pictures of laughter with all your best friends
projected upon the clouds in a dreamy orange sky

a timeline of lives that had been wonderfully lived
and of lives that fell into the unforgiving hands of death too soon
polaroids and candids taped upon the pages
with hand scribbled messages below

heaven's scrapbook grows day by day
as it acquires new lives to tell their stories
hidden within the stars that reside in the night sky
tied shut with ribbons of love

the lesson i never learned

sparks
flying
is
thrilling
until
you
get
burned

afterthought

i know
i'm not
your first choice
i know
i'm not
your one and only
trust me
i know
i see it
in the way you push me aside
in the way your eyes
look everywhere
but at me
in the way you flaunt me
to all your friends
but barely acknowledge me
when the crowd fades
i know
i'm just
an afterthought
the perfect accessory
to your
perfect
little
life

june

i thought
i lost you
but then
i realized
you can't
lose something
you never
had
in the first
place

a hill i will die on

to the
people
who say
girls
are more
complicated
than
boys
i
wholeheartedly
disagree
how can
we begin
to understand
what they want
when they
don't even know
what they want
when the mixed signals
and mind games
and cold shoulders
all seem worth it
for the seven seconds
they look at you
like
you're the center
of their
world
whether intentional
or accidental
stupidity
or arrogance
ignorance
or manipulation

they are a language
you've not only never heard of
but one that changes
its conventions
daily
at least my feelings
are written
all over my face
emotions injected
into my words
and actions
in an
oh so obvious manner
while they sit back
and disguise it all
with a shoulder shrug
or a smirk
a kiss
or twenty four hours
without a reply
a promise of a future
or an irish goodbye
entirely different actions
that might all mean
the exact same thing
or…
maybe not

happy i can't sleep

one of the best feelings
in the entire world
is
being so excited
you can't fall asleep at night
you just lay there
listening to the sound of your heart fluttering
unable to stop yourself from smiling
so many wonderful possibilities
floating around your head
so that the thought of sleep is nearly impossible
because
at that moment
your reality seems so much more
exciting
than your dreams

simply complicated

the reason boys
are so confusing
to girls
is that they can be so
simple
that we overthink
and over analyze
and over worry
finding a million ways
to interpret
their words
that mean nothing more
than the letters
forming them
it's the fact
that they are so simple
that makes them
so
freaking
complicated

knew this all along

you
were
not
a
sustainable

asterisk

you *give me butterflies

*gave

sweatshirt pockets

every little thing you do
i find to be the most interesting sight
i ever did witness
it doesn't matter what it is
you could just be standing there
with your hands in your sweatshirt pockets
talking to your friends
or listening to the music
blaring through your headphones
and i'd be mesmerized
it's as if every word you say
must mean something more
because it came from you
because you noticed me and
decided to grace me with your company
and i guess that's really all i want
to be seen by you
but more than that
to just be in your presence
to be around you
ridiculous
right?
i don't know
there's just something about the way
you make doing absolutely nothing
look so captivating
that gets me

black dress

the pain is different for us now
it's hitting you all at once
a torrential downpour with no warning
except the signs were alarmingly present
you just didn't tune into the forecast
i've been slowly grieving
slowly losing myself
for six months now
limbs like lead
as i went through the motions
and tried to force my feelings into hiding
disassociating
silently mourning
this is what gutted me
the words you spoke
that submerged me in icy cold water
shockingly cold
painful
but leaving me with remarkable clarity
this is the first time i ever thought i'd lose you
six months of pleas
and outward expressions
of what i need
what i want
how is it possible
this was the first moment it occurred to you
that i could leave
when i've been saying the same words
for months
the final weight that moved the scale
it appears to me
i bought the black dress
before we knew there would be a funeral to attend

free fall

have you ever fallen for someone
so hard
that it constantly feels like you're
free falling?

your stomach dropping
your heart beating rhythmically in your ears
your breath escaping your lungs
your mind just a blur of words and jumbled thoughts
and every emotion just feels so
powerful and real and raw
because right now
even though my feet are planted on the ground
i just keep falling

      and falling

       and falling

  deeper

  into

  you

people (don't) change

it's ironic
how people change when you don't want them to
they lose sight of who they are
and suddenly
the person you thought you knew better than anyone is
unrecognizable
but isn't it ironic
how people don't change when you need them to
when you're counting on it
when you're telling yourself that
this time it'll be different
but it's the same old game of chess
just with shinier pieces
i am told that
people change and
people don't change
depending on the situation
so which one is it?
you can't have your cake and eat it too
it can't be both
but then again
that's life for you
defying all the rules us humans must follow

falling anyway

i'm painfully aware
that i have much

f

   a

      r

       t

         h

           e

             r

to fall than you

the problem with being 18:

the problem with being 18 is that you feel everything to a much
greater extent

love gets you higher
pain cuts deeper

the highs are euphoric
exhilarating
intoxicatingly magical

but the lows hit so hard
like a train barreling through a person
who couldn't jump off the tracks
fast enough

you believe the highs are permanent
everlasting
so when they end,
it feels as if
you were blind sided
broken past the point of repair

so you then believe the same thing about the lows
that they are permanent
that they are everlasting

you haven't yet learned the temporary nature of life

and adults may roll their eyes
because they have the luxury of a birds eye view
of knowing the insignificance of the joys and pain
these moments will eventually have

but at 18

it hurts
and it's wonderful and carefree
but then it's overwhelmingly sad
so you're cautious
and you say you won't get your hopes up this time
but you already have
even though you know some things are too good to be true

because that's the other problem about being 18

you know the lesson
but you haven't learned it

so you listen to what everyone tells you
but their advice will almost always fall on deaf ears

because at 18
you take chances
you ignore the red flags
you trust the wrong people
you fall too fast and too deep
because in the moment
it looks good
it *feels* good

so hindsight is your worst enemy
you look back and wonder how you could be so stupid
how you didn't see it coming
but you can't blame yourself for not knowing better
when you didn't know better
for trusting the wolf in sheep's clothing

because at 18
you're not supposed to know better
you swing from one extreme to the other
chasing the next high

43

anticipating the next low

ever lonely, but ever hopeful

identity theft

i
miss
who
i
thought
you
were

november

a blank stare
is all
i can muster up today
standing in this room
filled with flowers
as people i don't know pass by to say they're *sorry*
it's not that i'm not feeling the emotions
it's that i am feeling them
so severely
it's as if i am being suffocated
like a scuba diver
who ran out of oxygen
i open my mouth to scream
but my lungs are filled with water
i am drowning
feeling everything
to such a great extent that
a blank stare
is all
i can muster up today
because the second that it falters
i will fall apart in front of all of these people
shattered into millions of pieces
like a broken stained glass window
so i drown silently
within myself
because it's easier than drowning in front of everyone
so no,
my blank stare does not mean i am unemotional
or cold
my blank stare
is the only thing keeping me from ripping open at the seams
the only thing keeping the flood inside of me
from destroying everything in its path

something special

i thought
we had
something
special
turns out
we had
nothing
at all

awe in his eyes

he
makes me feel new
makes me feel like
i'm something
special
a type of awe
in his eyes
when he looks at me
that makes feel like
a new version of myself
or maybe like the old
truest version
of myself
is finally reviving
herself because
he looks at me
like it's an honor
to know me
rather than an
expectation

things i told my mom about you

1. you were true to your word
2. you followed through on your promises
3. you knew what you wanted
4. you were genuine
5. you had good intentions
6. you never said anything you didn't mean
7. you were a good communicator
8. you were considerate of my feelings
9. you weren't like the other boys i'd fallen for
10. you would never hurt me
11. you weren't a player
12. you would never do to me what you did to her
13. you cared about me

things i told my mom about you that were actually true

life is a thief

i have
nothing
left to give today
but life keeps taking from me
i feel
so empty
so hollow
there is nothing left inside of me
blank pages
in an empty notebook
so much so i struggle to even
muster up the word *fine*
when someone asks me how i'm doing

gram

i wish
i would have known
that the last time
i hugged you
would be
the last time

mind vs. me

i feel like
we always know before our mind does
which i understand
sounds counterintuitive
aren't we the same as our minds?
sometimes i feel like we are
an entirely different being
our mind is complicated
producing an endless amount of thoughts
deceiving us
gaslighting us
but we are simple beings
all we want at the end of the day
is to be loved
and to be happy
it is our minds that complicate matters
and i feel like
we know much more than it likes us to believe
that feeling in the pit of our stomachs
telling us something is wrong
telling us when we've had enough
when it's time to walk away
we always seem to know before our mind does

lost cause

i'm a lost cause
circling through
a lost cause
lost with you

lived, but didn't learn

i'll crash and burn
they say you live and learn
but i'm falling into
the way things were before
counting the creaks
in the floor
praying to god i don't fall through
i try and tell myself
we don't do this anymore
but my mind has a mind of its own
and now i'm wondering
is it too soon
to call you and ask if you're okay
i know it's not my place
anymore
and the timing isn't great
but i've been waiting too long
to tell you how i've felt
ever since that day

to-do list

was
i
just
a
name
on
a
list
of
hearts
you
could
break?
check
me
off
your
lovely
little
to-do
list
because
this
is
done

wasted

1:00 a.m.
your name on my phone
even though
i haven't heard from you in weeks

i miss you
those words used to be enough

please don't disappear on me
those words had me hypnotized

i'm drunk
i know
because your ego is too high
when you're sober
and my first mistake was trusting
your drunken words

you always did know what to say
to keep me captivated
but nothing good comes from
drunk texts

and now my time
isn't the only thing
that's wasted

watch your step

watch your step
the sign said
but you tripped any way
fell down laughing as your eyes met mine

i wish you came with a warning like that
something that told me to stop
before i let myself fall
for a boy who's apathy hurt worse than his words did

a boy who would continually hurt me
but leave me begging for his attention

i wish you came with a warning sign
not that i would have read it if you did

i would have overlooked it just like you did that watch your step
sign

except my fall would be far more painful than yours

morning person

the stillness
of early mornings
moments
embedded between
layers of silence
sleep
still glossing over
your eyes
peace
before the world is
catapulted into the chaos
of daily life
your mind
at bay
in those first minutes
thoughts
as light as feathers
breath
slow and even
there's something
almost peaceful
about feeling
like you're the only person
in the
world
as if
the early mornings
existed
just for you

flower girl

she hands out
i love you's
like flower petals at a wedding
not because she doesn't mean them
not because she's fake or shallow
but because she needs something
to latch onto
i love you
is a promise
and promises can't be broken
or so she believes
she glanced at him
with her doe eyed stare
the extent of her purpose
her meaning
held in his eyes
his empty promises of forever
she believes them
because she needs to
because it's easier to deny than to feel
unwanted
he brushes her off like dust
gathering on a flat surface
he doesn't need to make excuses
she'll do that for him
because it's better to fill in the gaps with her own conjectures
than to look the truth in the eye
tape along the razor blade
to dull the ache
she'll stand by ever-loyal
ever-loving
like a child waiting for their parents to come home
she will wait for him
wait for the one rare moment when he pretends to see her

pretends to love her
to her, it will be worth it
because in that one moment
she will be able to fight off her fears
the loneliness embedded
deep into her soul
he will give her that reassurance
for a split second
but the clock's hands never linger on the same moment too long
and the fall will crash harder than the high
she accepts his coldness
his cruelty
because she needs him to prove them wrong
to prove herself wrong
that she isn't unwanted or unloved
even though she feels it in her gut
the haunting melody that floats through her mind
but maybe it isn't that she is unwanted
or unloved
it's that she's given her
i love you's
to people who do not love her in the passionate way she loves
them
people who do not deserve to love her
if only she saw how truly radiant and rare and beautiful she was
maybe then she'd hold onto her
i love you's
a little tighter
save them for someone
worthy of receiving them

butter fingers

i'm not looking for labels
to put a name to what we are
i'm not looking for long term commitment
or promises we're bound to break
i'm just looking for someone to talk to
to be there
long drives on empty roads
late night conversations that make the tired mornings worth it
scary movies
and sweatshirts that are too big but seem to fit better than my
own clothes
right, wrong, or indifferent
i'm not thinking of the future
i'm thinking of now
of what we could be in this moment
regardless of what's going to happen months down the line
i simply don't care
we only get to be young and stupid once
so if not now,
when?
because by playing it safe
busying ourselves with endless worries of tomorrow
haven't we already lost?
wasted time we could be begging for down the road
letting moments glide past us
without ever holding on tight enough
to catch them

so busy

i wish you would
stop
using *busy*
as an excuse
a reason to not give us a try
trust me
i've got *busy* down
if anyone understands *busy* it's me

sick of safe

sometimes i wonder if
your excuses and stupid games
are all because you're scared
scared to commit
or scared to try
scared to let yourself fall
scared for new beginnings
i don't know
it makes me wonder
if i'm not the only one who's scared
i just
express my fear
in a different way
or maybe i've decided
to stop latching onto scared
like a security blanket
knowing damn well
it's never going to get me anywhere
worth going

butterflies and heavy eyes

1:17 a.m.

butterflies

and heavy eyes

knowing how exhausted

i'll be in the morning

but recklessly unconcerned

if it means

talking to you

we went to church for you today

we went to church for you today
which is funny because you weren't very religious
i wore that black coat
the one i wore to your funeral
and haven't since
i felt no peace
from the service
no closure
and maybe that's just because
i'm still trying to figure out
what to believe in
so i cried in the car
on the way home
hoping there was something out there for you
that you didn't just disappear
into a vast and empty nothingness
that you were here
in some form
and i just had to be patient enough to see it
but i didn't
not then
not now
not ever
because you were no longer something i could see
but something i could feel
in between heartbeats
the warmth on cold november days
the flickers of memories pulsing through my head
i couldn't see you
no
but i could feel your presence
and for me
that was everything

just in case

the biggest difference between me and you is

i would never
treat someone i care about the way you treat me

whether you do it unintentionally
or not

i would never hurt someone
who continually stood by me,

even when i made their life a living hell

i would never place the games you do
send so many mixed signals
i've lost all sense of direction

killing me with your *maybe's* and *soon*
sharp blades that keep me from moving on

as if i am nothing more than convenience for you

a light to turn on when you need some attention
the girl who will always be there *just in case*

a prayer for rejection

you know
you've been hurt
when
rejection
is the most
comforting
option

i'm sorry

there's a difference
between
having feelings
for someone
and
wanting
to have feelings
for someone

collateral damage

pulled from the shadows
coated with a thick layer of darkness
she crawled into the tainted light
that shone harshly
and uncomfortably against her skin
as the crowds watched and analyzed
criticized and examined
they saw a girl who was stripped
of her childhood purity
weeping with the tears
of yesterday's faults
a girl who was programmed
to anticipate
the worst
a girl drowned in the panic
of a terrifying world
a girl who knew loneliness
as her only best friend
a girl rejecting her past
but afraid of tomorrow
found floating far from her identity
and like the bow on an unwanted present
she costumed it all with a large phony grin
collateral damage of an unkind world
but the people watched and laughed
at the odd damaged girl
and they wondered the origin of her demise
for they had but a clue
that she was a product
of them

battlefield

eventually
you realize
you're not fighting
a battle
against him
but against yourself
that he's just sitting back
watching you demolish yourself
waiting to see how far
you'll go
for him
and every once in a while he'll step into your aid
and the war will seem worth it
but
honey
it's not
you are fighting a war in which a part of you
will always lose
a war that will
always
leave him
unscathed

please don't push the red button

will you take
my broken pieces
and love
all of my
sharp edges
the parts of me
that he destroyed
decimated
with the push of his red button
unscathed
not me
apathy
was all his gain
my loss
of course
he couldn't help himself
couldn't help
but press the red button
and destroy
the most real thing
he's ever
known

self-worth

i
wasn't
even
worth
a
phone
call

october

for
someone
who
talks
so
much
you
sure
say
nothing
at
all

daylight savings

the end of
daylight savings
one less hour
today
i have
to think
about
you

my gold standard

give me a minute
before i fall back down

could you give me a minute?
because you've got me wrapped around

your finger
you linger
in the back of my mind

you're all of my bad habits
the reason why i'm sleep deprived

the gold standard of all my expectations

are you in love?
no
it's a complex situation

maybe i need a psych evaluation
to determine why i keep going down this path
the chase
the brokeness
the want what i can't have

every time it doesn't work out
i end up disappointed and sad

oh
i just keep ending up disappointed and sad

high school gymnasium

i know it's petty
but i pick her apart
as if it could get you to change your heart
but then you touch my hand
maybe it's innocent
but i can't
get you off my mind
keep crossing the line
a look across the room
four blue eyes
you smile
but it's breaking me inside
cause when it's all said and done
you're leaving with her
in the passenger seat
not me

i wish it was me

you can't sit here

the lunch rooms of my past are coming back to haunt me
just this time instead of the
round table
middle school
cafeterias
it's an overpacked
college
dining hall
where the conversations dance over my head
and i can't understand the inside jokes
because I wasn't there
when they were made
plans
past and future i am not a part of
and i am made painfully aware
that i am just tagging along
like the youngest sibling
the older ones never want to take
but are forced to by their parents
i try my best to contribute
i do
but soon i give up
and move my fork around my plate
without putting any food into my mouth
because i thought this could be a quick fix
slipping into a new group
but they are far too established
and i am far too out of the loop
i thought i had a solution
but really
all i had was a one night dinner plan
when there are nine lonely weeks left in the semester

off limits

stuck in my head
thought we were friends
when did it change?
why do i feel this way
about you?
and we're walking the line
wasting my time
but i'll do it for you
so text me good night
i'll get butterflies
but know it's not right
and nothing can fix it
because you're off limits

photographic memory

you told me once
that you have
a photographic memory
but yet
you can't seem to remember
anything you said to me
you made
so many promises
and so many plans
but
when it came time to deliver
you just…
forgot
that's talent
mr. photographic memory

ticket refund

you knew my weak spots
my faults
my achilles heels
used my own weapons
for your gain
but go ahead
play the innocent card
you didn't mean it
you didn't know what you were doing
is it easier that way?
remove the blame
pass it on
no remorse
no apology
and maybe in your head
you're the poor misunderstood hero
but that is a show
i will no longer buy tickets to

bottles

bottles of memories of you and me
bottles of love so pure
bottles of worries, anger, and fear
bottles of tears you cried

bottles of hope and bottles of prayers
bottles of time with you
bottles of pills
bottles of whispered words
bottles of oblivion too

there were bottles of pills on the bathroom counter
bottles i couldn't read
bottles i never understood the meaning of
bottles hindsight projected pictures of

bottles of love you got ready to leave behind
bottles of goodbyes you didn't want to say
bottles of hospital bills and treatments
bottles of goodbyes i couldn't predict

bottles and bottles of anger
bottles and bottles of tears
bottles and bottles of hope it wasn't true
bottles and bottles of longing for one more day with you

but you left me a small bottle
a bottle that once held pills
a bottle stamped with your name
a bottle that now held your small gold necklace
a bottle of promises to keep me safe
a bottle of our own special goodbye
a bottle connecting you and me

fine

i'm just trying to hide it
but my eyes aren't good at lying
you touch
my shoulder
and i blush
just a friend
just a crush
maybe you don't mean that much
your words,
they're about to cross the line

i'm fine

i'm fine

it's fine

pretty eyes white lies

pretty
eyes
white
lies
committed
the
perfect
crime
promise
i
won't
cry
but
you
escaped
just
fine

dodged a bullet

they say
i dodged
a bullet
so why
does
it feel
like i'm
bleeding?

talk is cheap, but time is not

talk is cheap
but your words to me
mean something
more than i can understand
lines are crossed
my mind is lost
give you the upper hand

my psychic said

smile of stone
but you nodded along
a pit in my gut
i knew it felt wrong
the thought took root
i hoped just a temporary stay
but once it slithered through the door
it wouldn't go away
my psychic said
the choice would have to be mine
i'm still angry that
you chose to pretend it was fine
but the eve of my birthday
which was the eve of our demise
the pictures show a light inside me
i hadn't seen in quite some time
it hurts me now to think
that conversation meant two different things
it was a shattering end for you
but it was merely my beginning

who's the bigger liar?

what's the use in drawing lines
if you just cross them all the time?
but when you ask i'll say i'm fine
i'll change myself
until you change your mind
can i blame you for lying
when i'm being this blind?
can't blame you for lying
when i'm lying to my own mind

dna

i was built to be broken
to get hurt
i guess it's in my blood
written into my dna
to give more than i have of myself
to fall
too hard
too fast
too deep

figure of speech

you're the best
is a figure of speech
but when
you said it to me
last night
it felt as if all the pieces
in the world
were clicking into place
the weight of what you were saying
washing over me
even though
i knew
deep down
it was nothing more
than a nicety

broke

if you put a price tag on my time
i'd be broke

because i bought in to your
i need you hoax

we went around in circles
but i thought we got away

now you leave me on open
because you have nothing left to say

tattoo

you traced the letters
of the new tattoo on my ribcage
with your fingers
slowly
softly
over my skin
i hope i never lose you
the lyric
now permanently etched on my body
a dark room
but i could make out the glow
of your eyes
as you read the line
and moved your fingers
to tilt my chin
up to face you
you said
i completely agree
i felt my breath hitch
in my throat
too much
too soon
i wish i caught it then
my apprehension
wish i listened
to the knots in my chest
instead of igniting a pattern
of always looking past the problem
always pretending
it wasn't that big of a deal
always making everything fine
even when i wasn't

same page different book

your ego
was as high
as my hopes
so
i crossed my heart
as you crossed your fingers
and said the prettiest words
smirk on your face
but not all that glitters is gold

and maybe promises are just shiny lies

and maybe words don't mean more than the mouth they come
out of

and maybe you can't be on the same page if you aren't reading
the same book

and maybe you were just a *player* in a game i didn't know i was
a part of

stop saying forever

forever
sounded so beautiful
rolling off your tongue
a promise
i knew better than to believe in
but i did anyway
because the thought of forever
with you
made my heart flutter
and my mind run wild
with the possibilities
of what we could be
a lifetime of stolen glances
and flushed cheeks
i should have known that
forever
had an expiration date
that before i even had a chance
to really get my hopes up
you would be promising
forever
to another girl

seventeen and cynical

love
is a made up word
a stupid string of letters
that makes people lose their minds
but what is love?
a title we bestow on relationships
a promise we fail to keep
i can love you
the same way you love her
and at the end of the day it doesn't mean anything
love isn't concrete
a tangible object we can hold on to
it is excuses
and emptiness
a term to define the feeling
of becoming so attached to someone
you feel as if you can't live without them
but you know what?
if love was so real
it would last
it wouldn't wither up like dying flowers
it wouldn't stain your hands like blood
it wouldn't leave you with so many broken pieces

seventeen and hopeful

take it one step at a time
but there's a fine line
between moving slow
and standing still
like dust collecting on a window sill
the world will spin
and years will go by
move forward
or get left behind
each step is progress
so don't look down
block out the sound of their voices
let your own music grace your ears
take the step, the jump, the leap
but don't let time's broom sweep
you off your feet
keep crawling, walking, running
whatever it may be
just keep moving forward
let life set you free

oh honey

i was the thrill once before
the girl who gave him butterflies
and left him stumbling over his words
he promised forever to me first
not that love cares about seniority
but i thought you should know
i was his world until you came around
and stole his attention like a crook
maybe you have feelings for him
or maybe it's a game to you too
but i see the way you look at him
stars in your doe-like eyes
i bet you believe him when he promises you the world
i bet you replay his compliments over and over in your head
he loved me too
we were supposed to last forever as well
but look at how long forever lasted us?
all of six months
oh honey
if you think you'll end up anything other than hurt
you're painfully mistaken
forever has a timestamp
and like the shiny new toy that becomes weathered with time
he'll find a new one to play with

catching feelings

sometimes
i wonder
if i mean anything to you
there's no way of knowing
how you feel
when you see my name flash across your phone screen
there's no way of knowing
if the thought of me gives you butterflies
that's the hardest part
of this whole
catching feelings thing
i know i'm letting myself fall
without any idea
of what's awaiting me
when i land

the lesson i never learned (part two)

falling
feels like
flying
until
you smack
the ground

i don't care

when i say *i don't care*
i really mean:

i care so much i'm trying to convince myself i don't so i don't end up disappointed

arm wrestling

sometimes i wonder
if we're both playing
the same game
if we both have feelings
for each other
but are too scared
to make the first move
it's like arm wrestling
both of us pushing
with the same force
neither of us willing to bend
because when you're playing
the same game
no one
is ever
going to win

hallway ghost

the shape of you is the same
all harsh lines and soft features
but i can feel the past five years worth of distance between us

you are like a figment of my imagination
blink
and i might miss you

a memory
a moment i've wanted for so long
but don't know what to do with now that i've caught it

i see you
but it isn't you

time has erased my place in your life
leaving me as nothing more than a mindless doodle
in the margins of an important paper

it's like my head no longer fits on your chest
with your chin on top
arms around my waist
like a lock and key

the shape of you is the same
but i no longer fit

maybe all we are is nostalgia wrapped feelings
and pain laced with lost time
love overtaken by circumstances
that don't seem all that important anymore

you know this feeling?

this
is the
worst feeling
thinking i had this
had you
just to feel it slip away
the uncertainty
gnawing at my insides
echoing in my mind
and i can't figure out
if i lost my chance
or if i ever had one
in the first place

missed opportunities

sometimes
i wonder
what would have happened
if things had been
different
if it weren't for
exes and best friends
who are now ex best friends
if it weren't for timing
and unaligned paths
if none of that mattered
would we have worked?
i think so
in a different world
in a different time
it would have been
us

in between

maybe
i'm just
a time filler
a hobby
to keep you busy
when you're bored
someone to fill the gaps
between
the moments
of your life

january

january is the fresh fallen snow
but
it is also the bleak grey mornings
that seem to stretch before me in
everlasting
g l o o m

a fresh start
renewal
reinvention
letting go

or 365 days of
disappointment
pain
and grief

sometimes
i wonder which one it is
ask me some other time, and my answer will change
often based on

you

the warm house,
the comforting fire
that burns me more than it brings light

january is the fresh fallen snow
cold and harsh
i draw a line in it
to separate this year from last
leaving the house and the fire behind
sacrificing the temporary comfort

the familiarity
for the inevitable burns that fade to scars
and make me forget the pain

but this time i can't forget

i draw the line in the snow
and begin to make the first footprints
in the white powder
while you stand unwavering
and unknowing

here's to letting go
whatever that may mean
the light switch flick from december to january
as if a single day will make a difference

congratulations

sometimes i worry
that if i start writing about you
i'll never stop
i know writing is supposed to be healing and all
but lately
all it does is dredge up memories of you
and send a storm of what if's into my mind
in the past
writing has been my way to cope
the one thing i can count on to make me feel better
so
congratulations
because breaking me wasn't enough
you had to go and ruin
my one way
to move on

the dictionary of you

the definition of what we were changed based on what was
convenient for you

what fit your agenda

if you crossed a line
it was fine
if you pulled back
that was fine, too

but me?
i was too cautious
or too emotional

too much, but not enough

you made the bold moves,
but i was too attached

you wanted the same things as i did
but said we were never on the same page from the beginning

a game always played on your terms
by your constantly changing rules
with a predetermined winner

the definition of what we were changed based on what was
convenient for you

an ever revolving dictionary
of razor sharp words
and beautiful lies

y.b.w.m (it's funny now)

i
will
never
listen
to
that
song
the
same
way
again

second hand smoke

i'm your ashtray
burn marks on my mind
from your cigarettes
too much smoke
swirling in the air to think straight
the flick of your lighter
and the world is bright
three seconds
eyes on mine
never long enough
until our world flashes black
again
you're gone
but still there
too far to hold
too close to forget
the burn comes slow
then all at once
darkness
and *pain pain pain*
addicted
you, to the nicotine of this game we play
me, to your second hand smoke

you

i can already tell
you're going to be
a problem

points for awareness?

red flags - i'm not ignoring them
no
i'm acknowledging their existence
neglecting their importance

i never claimed this was a good decision
it's about as stupid as decisions come

points for honesty?

i would love to say i debated it
i would love to say i had millions of good reasons for saying yes

but i only had one

~ you ~

closed not locked

i have never met a person who drives me crazier than you

a person who pushes all of my buttons at once

who makes me so frustrated
it feels like my entire body might ignite on fire

who annoys me to no end

who's redeeming qualities
don't make up for his shortcomings and mistakes

but they do

because if you were anyone else
i would hate you

but you're you

the only reason i'll ever need
the justification to every flaw
the explanation to why i will close the door
but never lock it

regret

none
of
this
would
have
happened
if
you
were
sober
that
night

the lesson i never learned (part three)

"did you *really* learn from what happened
or have you just not been presented
with an opportunity
to make a bad decision?"

someone asked me this the other day

i said of course i had learned
i had grown

you texted me that night

and there i was

reverting back to year old patterns
a cycle of butterflies
anticipation
subsequent disappointment

because you never could follow through

hesitation never crossed my mind

and like a moth captivated by the light
i crept closer and closer
to the fire that is you

always on the verge of comfortably warm

and burning into nothing but ashes

gasoline

you never change
but i never learn
the candle flickers
but it still burns
hands full of matches
words like nicotine
you might be the fire
but i'm the gasoline

the difference

red wine stains
the name on your lips
vanilla not rose
we notice the difference

like a canine searching for blood
on white dresses
wine or blood
it makes no difference

time weathered photographs
the new radiant version
me or her
do you notice the difference?

storms with a chance of vodka

a misstep
when the vodka hits
like an evening storm
sober thoughts
and drunken words
are one in the same
when the phone is so close
and the *why not's* have disappeared
almost as quickly as the contents of the bottle
you were a mistake
from start to finish
same as the first shot
and the fifth
but the burn and the high
blurred out my periphery
no past
no future
only now
so the alcohol on my tongue
speaks for me
and my desperate words fall into a void
of thoughts better left unsaid
and mistakes better left unmade
because soon enough
you will be no different
than the last shot of vodka
i will regret you both
the same

dry january

across a table
if you were a drink
i'd be 21 days sober
the bottle poised in front of me

my car is a time machine

take a step
take it back
your words were always made of glass
edges sharp as knives
as lies
as you

boy with the deceitful eyes
in the end he me made me cry
did anyone see
it going differently?

now every road in this town
is a time machine to him
and all those songs i used to play
are permanently ruined

the snow is falling down
but i feel like its june
on the way home from the party
i was mesmerized by you
and all the lines i crossed
for the sake of winning your heart
but the only thing i gained
was a mind full of scars
because you never really cared
and i was ill prepared
for a lesson learned in time
in lies
in lines

so no i'm not crying
i just miss you
sometimes

bit by bit

she bites her lip when she's nervous
and wishes on angel numbers
even when she knows it's pointless
and luck is never on her side

she can't keep her nails painted for too long
because she chips away at the polish
bit by bit until there is nothing left
just like the world does to her

she says she doesn't care
but she does
and even though she knows it's pathetic
she can't keep her lonely heart from hoping

she wears smiles like masks
slips them on with ease
whenever someone enters the room
because that is what is expected of her

she listens to your problems
even when her mind feels like shattered glass
and the weight of her unspoken words feel like they might
consume her
because that's what you want from her

she believes his promises
and turns a blind eye to the red flags on rocky waters
because that's what he wants her to do
and for the hope of him, she must play the role

she takes things personally
even when she shouldn't but she can't help it
and everyone rolls their eyes

because they just don't understand

she feels powerless in an unforgiving landscape
that chips away at her bit by bit
until day by day she loses herself
to the wants of the world

he is.

he is a cup of black coffee.
too strong.
too bitter.
he is red wine on white clothes.
a stain you can't remove.
he is ocean water in april.
a cold you aren't ready for.
but he is also bonfires in january.
a warmth that makes you forget it's the dead of winter.

old doors

old ways
won't open
new doors
but what if i just want to go back
through the old doors
with their broken handles
and cracking paint
and familiarity
i don't want changed habits
or fresh perspectives
new keys that will never fit right
because i want my old ways
which will lead me
through my old doors
which will lead me
to you

wish u the best

i don't wish you the best
it's the nice thing to say when a relationship ends
the mature thing
but isn't lying just as immature?
when you cross my mind
all i can think is
i hope someone hurts you the way you hurt me
i hope that you experience that at least once
to feel like you're constantly playing a game
where you are always the designated loser
i hope you fall too hard into someone's empty promises
and hang onto every fool's gold words they say
and i hope you watch it fall apart
shatter like a glass falling to the ground in slow motion
while there is nothing you can do to stop it
i hope you blame yourself
and wonder where you went wrong
i hope you spend a few weeks overanalyzing every single
moment
picking apart any split second you could have messed up
spending every sleepless night replaying scenes
and wishing you could make a different choice
thinking that if you were good enough
it wouldn't have gone this way
i hope she doesn't even give you the opportunity for closure
for a goodbye
for ending things the right way
and leaves you hanging in limbo
because you weren't even worth a phone call to her
i hope you feel absolutely miserable
and then i hope you see me in passing one day
when you are as irrelevant to me as a speck of paint on a wall
and you see for the first time
the weight of your actions

of the *have it all*
better than everything
mentality you had
i hope you feel an inescapable guilt burrowing inside of you
that no matter how fast you run
you just can't get away from
i hope the smallest part of you misses me
and wonders what it would have been like
if *you* had been different
so no
i don't wish you the best
i wish you an opportunity to learn
to be a better person
because take it from me firsthand
some lessons
can only be learned the hard way

fever dream

your mouth tasted like weed
and your hands found my hair
the party was too hot and too loud
but the walk back was too cold
despite the butterflies in my stomach
that were fluttering too wildly
making me shiver even once i was inside
the blue lights disguised the fact it was almost three
and there was too much at stake
even though it should have meant nothing at all
but you talked about your dad and the pressure
and the window overlooking the road
and how you like to watch the cars drive by
and the leaves in the fall
and i'd be lying if i said i didn't melt
because i started falling right there
too hard and too fast for my own liking
and now i'm too restless and too anxious
a saturday night in february that was too unexpected
a moment i hope
more than i'll ever admit
i'll get back

credit where credit is due

if i could ride out this high
i think i'd be fine
in a couple days time
if you could take it all back
would i take you back
is the question worth the answer when
you think you're right
and i'm the bad guy
we'd spin in circles until we're flying
so check back in a day
because i've lost my way
home was your face
and now i've got nowhere to fall
i can't give you credit for much
but for breaking me down
you deserve it all

earthquake

being with you was like walking along tectonic plates

steady ground
beautiful skies
step after step
thinking i could do this for the rest of my life

until the ground started to shake
booming
rumbling
destroying
everything into nothing
the perfect picture
disintegrating into dust

your fault lines were always there
i just couldn't see them

band-aids and bullet holes

you're a
temporary solution
to a problem
i can't solve

deal?

you're holding the matches
but i'm putting out the fires
toxic attachment
because you're such a pretty liar
you know
i'd fall from grace
for you
and i know
you wouldn't stop me
would you?
you don't want me like i need you
but i'm addicted
so i'll cling to it
breathless
and i'm desperate
for the day you'll change your mind
i say i'm not trying to fix you
but that's exactly what i want to do
so pretend you love me tonight
and i'll pretend i don't see the lie
written in your eyes

baseball

i used to watch the red sox play
so i'd have something to talk to you about
no i didn't care how many RBI's so-in-so had
i didn't even know what an RBI was
but i talked about it like i knew every statistic
of every game ever played
because you talked with your hands
and your expressive eyes
you loved the game
so i wanted to love it to
because honestly
i just wanted to be someone you wanted
at night
when you asked me if i was watching the game
i wasn't
but i'd turn my tv from grey's anatomy to baseball
and send you a picture
because you would always say you were proud
and we'd talk about the game in real time
as it was happening
those nights were the best
they made me wonder what it would be like
to actually watch a game with you
what it would be like
to mean something to you
but in the end
all i gained
was a mind full of useless baseball knowledge
i don't think i'll ever need

tag you're it

you're
my
favorite
game
to
play

nonexistent

can someone tell me why
i still miss you
sometimes
why it stings
like fingers plucking
guitar strings
minor chords
on piano keys
can someone tell me why it hurts
when i see
a picture of you
wondering if you hate me
or if you still think about me too
i have conflicted visions
in my head of you
when i get like this
i don't know how to feel
because the person i'm missing
was never real

starry eyes

desperate heart
starry eyes
she fell for a guy
who said he loved her
and then changed his mind

tuesday

freshmen year of college
it's tuesday morning
but my heart longs for friday afternoon
just not in the same way as before
frat parties
and cheap vodka
a series of wild nights
before the week repeats itself
instead
i can't wait to go home
i don't mean it as a figure of speech
my stomach feels sick
and my restless legs tap the floor
fervently
my mind is filled with images of my mother's car
pulling up on the side of my dorm room building
i can see myself sliding into the safety
of the passenger seat
being whisked away
to a magical land called *home*
where the problems of this campus
are less pressing
less soul crushing
but i know i've been reliant
on that unsustainable solution
a cop out that is acceptable
for the first week
or two
but not the fifth
so i'll have to wait for friday
even though that is also a temporary solution
to a long term problem
in the meantime
i make a list in my head of all the ways i can occupy my time

knowing the list will never take up enough of it
to distract me
from my thoughts

the ledge

my lip trembles
but i stare aimlessly out the car window
because for some reason
in my mind
i thought
spring break would last forever
but now i'm back here
the car making a sharp left
at the stoplight
before last week
it was just about
"getting to spring break"
and when i made it
i felt the biggest sense of relief
rebuilding?
moving forward?
that was to be accomplished after
well,
now it's after
and i don't feel like i have it in me to stay
but don't have the capacity to understand
what calling it quits means
so i stare absentmindedly
out the window
while my mother tells me i can do this
i know i can
the question is
do i want to?

fifteen

you made me feel fifteen again
in the best and worst way

words

i am a person of words
i choose mine carefully
because i understand their meaning
their weight
their impact

your voice weaponizes words
you use them to hurt me
in the places you know will cut
the deepest
and you shrug it off
as if it isn't a big deal
as if i am being too sensitive

maybe that is because you do not understand
the power of language
which is ironic for someone
in a major dependent upon it
you're blind to
the way in which words can break and destroy
that is not an excuse
but a sign of ignorance
of cruelty
the way your hurl insults
like daggers
at someone you once called
your best friend

i am rational and thoughtful
it's why i am a person of words
why i choose mine carefully
you are a person of hate
of anger
of resentment

139

your words reflect that
the malice of them
burning in your eyes

unwritten rules

i play it safe
you play it cool
abiding by all of our
unwritten rules

watching movies (yeah sure)

not that you were wondering
but
i was never
watching the movie
just
sitting there
waiting
for you
to make
the first
move

words in an old notebook i found when i came home from college

gas prices are too high
but i still go for two hour drives
how else am i supposed to get you off my mind?
my best friend in the passenger seat
drowning ourselves in music's misery
maybe i'll just drive down his street
so i'll hit the gas
and speed towards
a street lined with red flags
and red lights
but i blew past all the stop signs
so i crossed my fingers
as you crossed my heart
held onto your *maybe's*
until i fell apart
you're the worst of my bad habits
but i can't find the brakes
because it's you
the choice i'll always make
nevermind
just take a left turn please
but my friend says *no*
don't drive down his street

it's just us

i feel like
i get
to see
a side of you
that no one else
does
i feel like you've
shown me
who you are -
the real you
that you trust me
that you feel
safe enough with me
to show me
not just the good parts
but the things you struggle with
the thoughts that
keep you awake
at night
i feel almost honored
special
that you chose
to open up
to me
that i get
to see the sides
of you
that you keep hidden
from the rest of the world
and
if you ask me
it's all of those things -
the weight you carry on your shoulders
the worries you have

your baggage
that make me like you
even more
how lucky am i
to have been brought
into your world
to know you
the way most people don't
or won't
ever
get the chance to

safe place

in the midst of all the chaos
of all the horrible things
this world
has recently
provided me with
i find you
my safe place to land
or in this case
crash
because i am spiraling
out of control
but there you are
catching me
as i fall
bringing me
peace of mind
during these
difficult times

it wasn't fine

settled for mediocre
now i'm ripping off my nails
staring blankly into nothing
we were always bound to fail

i'm kind of thinking i grieved us
long before we were this far gone
disassociated went through the motions
but how couldn't you tell something was wrong?

wasn't it wrong
me crying every time
wasn't it wrong
me managing your life
wasn't it wrong
you saying it's fine
saying we're fine
when you knew i was dying
saying it's fine
saying we're fine
were you even trying
saying it's fine
saying we're fine
did you know you were lying

withdrawal

i
miss
the
sound
of
your
voice
like
an
addict
misses
a
drug

sunday mornings at the kuhn's

fifties music
playing from the speaker
the living room
recapping the night before
over coffee
a mismatched collection
of mugs
from trips sprawling the years
sun reflecting
off the window
filling the house
with a golden
glow
football sheets
and game day predictions
interrupting morning activities
with the occasional
dance move
all smiles
and laughter
grateful to be
a part of a family
that loves
as hard as
this one

sunday nights at the kuhn's

late night
bowls of ice cream
lights dimmed
music
turned up as high
as it can go
meaningful lyrics
interwoven with memories
this is the moment i realized i loved your dad
mom says
through teary eyes
find the meaning in the words
dad says
as we
cheers
our glasses
sunday night football
and home cooked meals
dancing
in the dark kitchen
advice
honest, but heartfelt
a safe place
in the storm
that is life
deep conversations
and singing
at the top of our lungs
grateful to be
a part of a family
that loves
as hard as
this one

those words

i would be lying if i said
those words
hadn't crossed my mind
if i said they weren't on the tip of my tongue
threatening to slip out
as you looked deep into my eyes and said
have they always been this blue?
and tilted my chin upwards
ever so slightly
so that my lips
could meet yours
if i said those words weren't pounding
with every thrum of my heartbeat
if i said they weren't begging
to be released
when you held me tight
and asked me what i was thinking about
i lied and said nothing
nothing
nothing
nothing
and maybe that was almost true
because
i was thinking about nothing
nothing other than how much
i wanted to say
those words
to you

he stayed…i didn't

i've never held on tighter
arms around you in a way that said
i'll never let you go
because you were gone for so long
i could feel the longing
in the pit of my stomach
in the heaviness in my chest
but i'm here now
you said
i'm here with you
and somehow
i fell harder
and i held on tighter
and you kissed me in a way that said
i missed you
and the look in your beautiful eyes
and the strength of your arms around me said
i don't want to lose you
and you're here now
you reminded me
you're here
please stay

words he never said

i don't know what's worse

the words you said

or the ones you didn't

on the verge of february

the ground is a thick layer of ice
frozen by the cold words dripping from my mouth
but how sharp is the edge
that's been fine tuning itself for months
with each tear dripping from my heavy eyelids
and every word that never burrowed deep enough into your skin
the knots in my stomach
don't lie like my mind does
when it says that fine and safe may be okay
when i sacrifice the present version of myself
for a hypothetical chance of a future
i thought was carved into stone
a blood oath at nineteen
that never was so
realized as the fog cleared on the windshield
that the people pleaser in me must be laid to rest
must be stopped from spreading lies
and building cages around me
so maybe the voice escaping now is cold
but it has remained unheard
left to sharpen in barren darkness
shaking but finally truthful
in knowing its edges must cut the safety net
we've grown far too accustomed to

wine drunk on the fourth of july

wine drunk
lying on my bedroom floor
time warp
waiting for your
name on my phone
your arms around me
overthinking every
word i said
and every word you didn't
do you still miss me?
staring at the ceiling
i'll keep staring at the ceiling
letting it consume me
it's different this time
so why is it *not* different this time

a beautiful birthday

a beautiful birthday
is what the card said
exchanged in the front seat of my car
after a lunch of feigning smiles
and gut feelings
it broke me to come to terms with
the distance between us felt
like something you could reach out and touch
at least it did for me
sick to my stomach
and the heaviness in my chest
as i opened the carefully selected gift
and knew in my heart
the choice i was ready to make
a beautiful birthday
yes
beautifully painful
beautifully tragic
perhaps
beautifully free

it ends at the beginning

it seems fitting
this new chapter begins
the way the last one ended
with conversations in parked cars
fighting to close the book
but it kept springing open
because the most meaningful
and heartbreaking
moments
seem to occur
in unmoving vehicles
which
is where you kissed me
when our song was playing
in the background
and where i put myself first
and severed our ties
so this new chapter could begin
just as the last one
started
just as the last one
ended
because maybe beginnings and ends
are no different
maybe they're so deeply intertwined
it's impossible to separate them
to move forward
we must meet ourselves
at the start
because for me
it begins and ends in the same place
with conversations in parked cars

no one's wife, no one's mother

i'm no one's wife
and no one's mother
so why have i been
someone's wife
someone's mother
carrying the weight of problems
that aren't mine
managing a life
that isn't mine
the expectation
that i would always swoop in
to fix it
laying myself down
to become everything and anything you need
at any given moment
no spark
no thrill
a dependence on me
i can't enable any longer
feeling stuck like a forty year old woman
in a marriage she settled for
but
i'm twenty one
and i'm not
someone's wife
someone's mother
i can't be
so i won't be
i'm sorry
no
i can't be sorry
for putting myself first
for following what i want
so i won't be

i won't be sorry
i won't be someone's wife
i won't be someone's mother

cosmic

the timing of this
makes me feel like
the universe was attempting to get in touch with me
attempting to send a sign
and maybe i'm delusional
for thinking that sign
was in the form of
a six foot tall
man
but i'm the type
that would take that
and run
but the night felt supercharged
cosmic energy
radiating between us
spark to fire
ease to excitement
unexpected
in every sense of the word
this feels lucky
you said
and in fact
it was
feeling free for the first time in months
and there you were
at a place we've both been before
but never crossed paths
until this night
this
lucky
lucky
night
i can't help but think the universe concocted

halfway to heartbreak

love is
halfway to heartbreak
isn't it?
there's two decisions
to be
and to end
so once you've decided
to be
isn't there only one choice
left to make
the choice to be
together
is the halfway point
between
the beginning
and the end
whether that end is
tomorrow
a month
a year
fifty years
natural
or mutual
or one-sided
love is
halfway to heartbreak
but maybe
i'm okay
with that

dating in this decade

i miss
the updates you'd give me on your day
what you were doing
how you were feeling
the questions you'd ask about mine
i miss
coming home
and falling into your words
our late night conversations
that made it feel
like we existed
in a world
all of our own

i'm scared

scared
because
i think i know where i want this to go
nevermind
i know where i'm going to want this to go
existing in this space of time
i'm at ease
smiling at my phone as i walk to class
thinking about you
like i'm fifteen again
i know in a few weeks what i'll be wanting
and it was never a part of my plan
but with the way my plans keep falling apart
it seems
it's time
to let the universe take the reigns of control
but i'm scared
for the almost instantaneous shattering
of my cool girl wild fun era
that never quite was
scared of caring
so i pretend i don't
when i already do
but i'll push it off
and just be
because
it seems
as if the universe
had a plan of its own

roses and stones

the roses catch my tears
black mascara filled
holding them like fresh drops of dew
petals deep red like a bottle of fine wine
i lay them down sweetly
against the cold stone
so they can sleep soundly
where my heart lays forevermore

spotify

ooh
when the breakup playlist
becomes a crush playlist
no one listening will understand
but me
and even i
don't really understand
it's just that this timing
makes my head spin
but yet
makes perfect sense
so the breakup playlist
is *s l o w l y*
leaning towards a
stupidly falling
stupidly complicated
stupidly freeing
combination of lyrics
that should make sad
but really just
make me
smile

phoenix

it's quite clear now
he was my joe alwyn
slowly killing me
with his inability
to listen despite the hundreds of pleading conversations
to change despite his promise to
his dependence
became a cage
i didn't know i was locked in
until i was free
but now the boy sitting next to me
stares at me with a glow in his eyes and says
i'm free spirited
i'm extroverted
i'm exciting
he sees a version of me i haven't felt like in so long
a version of me that is beginning to seep through
a version i realize i miss
it was then i saw the wrought iron bars of the cage
and decided the phoenix wings on my back
were not broken
but merely rusty
it was then i rose
and flew
and reflected
and knew
i would never wear a man's initial around my neck again
never stand for *i don't know's*
never ignore the searing
roaring
feeling
in my gut
never look someone in the eye
who pretended they couldn't see

the way their
reliant clinging
was breaking me
until i was only skin and bones
going through the motions
and he still asked *why*
still said
this was the first time i thought i'd lose you
when the arguments
and outward pleas
had been occurring for more than six months
so i stepped off the pedestal he put me on
and vowed to never return
and it only occurred to me once i was
flying
that i hadn't been me in so long
had let him dull
the passion
and energy
and light
burning inside me
but now the boy sitting next to me says
i'm free spirited
and fun
and exciting
and smart
and he listens
and he sees me
truly me
but more importantly
i'm listening to me
to my needs
to the intuition whispering softly in my ears
and i see me
and i know
this loss

is the reason
i found myself
so i vow now to
never lose me again
to never leave me again
i will remember
the unbreakable wings
ready to shatter
the glass ceiling

new study

attention
attention
new study finds
all men
have
split personality disorder
hope this helps
!!!

MY MUSIC

stop
stealing
my
music
sabrina
didn't
write
that
song
for
you

hush

hush
said the woman
we were ever so quiet
as we tiptoed through
the graveyard
following the pack
of elegantly dressed people
who could have passed as gala attendees
to the stone
we were told to say our farewells
and let time fade
our tears
into happy memories
an over inflation of its powers
in my opinion
the sky was the most depressing
shade of grey
as if it too
were in mourning
the men in their suits
hung their heads
as the women in their clicking high heels
wept
i felt the lump in my throat grow
and my blood run bitter cold
from the sky's tears
i knelt in front of the grave
a living breathing person
turned into nothing more than a lousy stone
she wasn't given a fair trial
in death's courtroom
but i knelt anyway
feeling the dirt rubbing against my knees
 and with hunched shoulders

i cried
i cried
and i cried
until i felt a soft pat on my back
and a woman's soft voice whisper
hush
but when i turned around
there was no one there
but me
no one but me
and the stone

cool girl

i'm trying to be the cool girl
but a cool girl
would never say
she's trying to be a cool girl
and i am inherently built to care
just a little too much
especially when your words
draw me in
like they do
the gentle lull of the ocean
pulling me in
until they push me back out
because i said a little too much
but did i really say too much
when we take into account all your
i miss you's
and
i can't stop thinking of you's
but i'm being cool
i swear
i can be
a
cool
cool
girl

u up?

this text
made me think more
than my last
exam
did
just after midnight
you said
my name
written with an extra e
like you tend to do
hi
u up?
now i'm kicking myself
for falling asleep
wondering
what you wanted to say
i've spent more time today
debating all the possibilities
of
what you might have meant
as if it were
a physics problem set
comparing answers with my friends
re-doing the work
over and over
still not sure if i got it right
until i realized
i spent more energy
today
decoding
three meaningless letters
than i did
taking my last exam

just one bad day

i have more bad days than good days
but i still find myself saying
"it's just one bad day"
as an excuse to those around me
as if it is the exception
rather than the rule
i wonder at what point
the tears
and aching feeling in the pit of my stomach
will have caused the validity
of that statement
to implode
to become as meaningless
as this life can seem
so i'll still call my mom
from my empty dorm room
fighting the quiver in my voice
and say
"it's just one bad day"
while we both pretend to ignore
that those were the same words
i uttered yesterday
and the day before
and the day before
and the day before

hope

hope is the little voice
in the back of the room
often soft
and shaky
but if you listen
you can hear it
echoing in the loud and crowded spaces
the last man standing
when all else has been abandoned
it is the light switch
in the darkness
the flower
budding after the bitter cold
like the crest of a wave
flowing like the lyrics of a song
like a mother
calming her crying child
it is the lullaby
and the rally cry
hope is the little voice
in the back of the room
often soft
but always there

i'm writing again

when people ask me
how i know
if i made
the right decision
i say
i'm writing again
it's not
only that i'm writing again
but that i can't stop
it's how i know
the weight of the situation
was a heaviness in my chest
a blockade
to the words spiraling in my mind
begging to be released
but now
they're flowing freely
months and months of words
i was too scared
to speak
into existence
throughout my life
i've always known
i made the right decision
if after i made it
i throw myself
into my writing
again

drunk text?

is getting a drunk text a good sign?
does it mean
you were thinking of me
late last night
when the alcohol hit
just a little too hard
does that mean
i'm on your mind
does that mean
when you've lost your inhibitions
it's me you want to talk to
or
was it just random
something you thought of
because you were bored
i like to think not
especially as i smiled
at my phone
this morning
and wondered
if you were thinking of me
like i've been thinking of you
so a drunk text is a good thing?
question mark?

devil's in the details

walking
and it catches me off guard
makes me melt
the way your arm slides around me
present in the moment
not thinking
but thinking so damn much
easy
but as if you've been waiting
and couldn't hold back any longer
the simple gesture sets my skin on fire
as you laugh
about my ripped jeans
bare knees
falling victim to february's harshness
i look down at your
blue new balances
on dark icy roads
your corduroy jacket
my leather jacket
i like the aesthetic
your aesthetic
our aesthetic
especially as you lead me inside the bar
it feels special
like *we're* special
especially as your friends
look at us with a bit of awe
they smile and whisper in my ear
about how excited they are
how excited *you* are
they tell me all the things you've said about me
how unexpected this is
i keep hearing that

unexpected
but in the best way
you just fit
the girl next to me says
and throughout the night
you periodically
put your hand on my shoulder
laughing
bantering back and forth
you took my hands
and said
you were ready to go whenever
and i'd be lying
if i said i wasn't thrilled
to be leaving with you
feeling more spark
more excitement
than i have in months
saying goodbye
to your smiling friends
hand on my back
as you followed me out
corduroy jacket
leather jacket
blue new balances
pink gazelles
is it wrong
to say
i felt like we were
celebrities?

call your mom

freshmen year of college
i learned the importance of the phrase *call your mom*

when i left for school in august
my mom told me she was always only a phone call away
a comment she may have regretted making
because i took her up on that offer
in any and every way i possibly could
no matter the circumstances or situation
she was always my first call
my favorite call
we would joke that at school
we talked even more than when i was at home
due to the sheer number of phone calls
i made to her each day
thank god we don't live in a time
where you have to pay for minutes
because we both would be in debt

i called her anytime i was walking anywhere alone.

i called her when i was sad and missing home.

i called her when i just wanted to hear her voice
to be reminded of being back at our house
talking at the counter while i did homework
and she cooked dinner.

i called her to help me study for a test.

i called her when i was convinced i failed said test.

i called her when it turned out i scored a 98 on said test
and in fact did not fail.

i called her to tell her about the new friends i made.

i called her to gossip about new boys i thought were cute.

i called her for advice when i needed it most.

i called and got advice when i didn't want to hear it.

i called when my world was shattering and needed to come home.

i called when i returned to school
and needed her encouragement to get me through the day.

i called when i was lonely and wanted someone to talk to.

i called to ask questions.

i called to find answers.

i called laughing.

i called crying.

i called when everything was going great.

i called when things weren't so good.

i called to help figure out
what outfit i should wear
and what i should eat for dinner
and where should i park because the lot was full
questions she would laugh at and say
how am I supposed to know that?

i called when i was in a crisis that wasn't really a crisis
and when i was in one that carried a little more weight.

i called her to share every bit of good news
and every piece of bad news too.

i called because she is not just my mom
but my person
my best friend.

50 / 50

my gut feeling
tells me
there's no in between
you will either be
the best decision
or
the worst decision
of my
life

super power

i'm always trying to manipulate time
latching onto it
with a white knuckled grip
to hold it back
from moving forward too fast
then staring aimlessly at clock
as if my mind can will it to speed faster
i wanted this power at fifteen
and i want it now
but when will i learn
time
will bend to no one's will
let alone mine
when will i learn
to live
in the present
and let time swoop me up in its whirlwind
as fast
or
as slow
as it pleases
but yet i can't seem to stop
wishing
for more time
or
less time
can't seem to stop
holding on
while simultaneously
rushing
to let go

rise

the challenge
will never
shrink
itself
to meet you
you
have to
rise
to meet
it

i'm a contradiction

when he gives
too much
i don't want it
when he gives
me nothing
i'm begging
for more

pizza at the counter

my dad and i have the same nose
we also think the same way
we're soft spoken
but we love meeting new people
ever since i was young
he was the type of parent
who let me make mistakes
let me figure it out on my own
but was always there
to soften the blow of the fall
to offer quiet advice
subtly slipping it in
simple but profound
he's a man of actions
i once mentioned i wanted soft pretzels
and he spent an entire afternoon
scouring martha's vineyard
until he found them
he makes the drive up to my school
to see me every so often
my apartment doesn't have laundry
so he picks mine up and returns it to me
we eat pizza at a spot downtown
we talk about hockey
and updates on a trial we both follow
he reminds me to breathe
to not take it all so seriously
he checks in
in his own quiet way
and i'm not sure if he realizes
but those moments
eating pizza with him at the counter
keep me grounded
a sliver of peace in the chaos

high speed train

high
low
can't find my middle ground
high
low
sanity's nowhere to be found
at ease
only when you're texting me
but even then
i'm high
which is the same as being
low
and i know
i should be focusing
on me
but i'm always on
a moving train
and i fear
i'm barreling through
chaos
headed for disappointment
all in the name of
fun

forever: the meaningless word

forever
is one of those words
we use
and overuse
we promise it
and inevitably undermine it
until the word is
hollow
from a bird's eye view
we say we should ban
the word
and stop making
such arbitrary oaths
but i've said that word
meant it, too
and then i watched
as it became
stripped
of its meaning
because
perhaps forever
is something
we can only commit to
for a season
some much longer than others
perhaps forever
is a feeling
a feeling of connection so strong
with another person
it seems at that moment
that you could bask in it
for the rest of your life
but we don't know
what we don't know

and time
and unforeseen circumstances
shift the definition
of the word
we pass out
like candy
which sounds like a lie
but perhaps it is merely
a string of letters
we place too much stake in
a string of letters
we place on a pedestal of permanency
when we should
honor
its
temporary nature

true colors

feeling blue
once in a blue moon
when the white lies
color me grey
the black sheep
broke the golden rule
i tried
i tried
to play it cool
but i was seeing red
then blacking out
blood stained hands
it's obvious now
i was green with envy
waiting for your green light
stuck at a yellow
the permanent type
you paint the town red
which paints me quite grey
until your golden light turns on me
tell me you're here to stay
you were out of the blue
now i'm lost in the grey
together we're golden
where do your true colors lay?

figure of speech (part two)

i can't stop thinking about you
was just a phrase
until it was overwhelmingly true
until yesterday with you
because the only thoughts
moving through my head
are flashes of moments
and words you said
words i'm already begging
to hear again
disassociated from time
in a fever dream state
does this make you mine?
i can't stop replaying
the moment from each angle
recapping at my kitchen table
nonverbal in the car
because my mind's stuck in a loop
i can't stop thinking about you
was just a figure of speech
until it was about you

unexpected

you were not
supposed to happen
not in that way
not at that time
but hey
i'm so glad you did :)

psa: it's never different

they say you lose them how you get them
but i thought this was different
i thought i was different

...

i thought *you* were different

never been cool

hope
leads to
disappointment
the same way
catching feelings
leads to
hurt
i say i don't care
but the flutter in my chest
and the excited nerves in my stomach
tell a different story
shattering
the *play it cool* vibe
i'm trying to hold onto
like glass

treading water

my fault
for saying yes in a heartbeat
your fault
for asking when you knew i couldn't say no
because you knew
didn't you
knew the toll it was taking on me
treading water
with two bodies
instead of one
knew if you shed a few tears
i'd do anything
even drown myself
to keep you afloat
laying problems at my feet
making me feel like
my leaving would destroy you
even though
my staying was destroying me

words i can't forget

you peak my stress levels
but you brought me back to life
in the moments where you whisper
i got you
you say my name
and tell me to trust you
but i have a tendency to overthink
a tendency to look too far ahead
you have a tendency to run
or so i've heard
so i've seen
but you walked back through my door
the flaws are not lost on me
but neither is the fact that you came back
we talked it through
that's new for me
i think it is for you too
you cause chaos my friends have to smooth over
but you ease the chaos in my life too
you're a contradiction
but so am i
both of us a mosaic of broken pieces
you wear your baggage like the perfect pair of jeans
i hide mine behind sad music and bouts of productivity
i think you're a lesson
to teach me to stop overthinking
to allow myself to truly and fully have fun
we're more than a coincidence
more than a case of
right place
right time
it feels like there were too many choices
that had to be made
in such a precise way

for our timing to line up like it did
for it not to written in the universe's
pages of plans
but that could be delusion speaking
my hope for this working out
is manifesting as a self proclaimed ability to predict the future
but i know a thing or two about gut feelings
i know they don't usually steer you wrong
and since the moment we met
some all consuming premonition told me
this wouldn't be easy
but that someway
somehow
it would be worth it
so right now
i'm living for the quiet moments
where it's just you and me
conversation flowing with ease
and for the first time
i'm feeling free even with someone next to me
the way you look at me makes me feel brand new
more alive than i think i might ever be
despite everyone's hesitation
i'm holding onto the words you whisper
when no one else is around
i won't hurt you
i got you
trust me
i didn't say it that night but wanted to
the fear overtook my want
because this feels like a piece of stained glass
previously broken
but beautiful when put back together
smoothing out each other's edges
fragile but hopeful
in a way no one understands

i tread lightly
because i don't want to mess this up
even though we both already have
even though we both will again
so consider this my way of telling you
i won't hurt you
i got you
trust me

a lesson i learned

heartbreak
noun

- broken glass

time
noun

- the sandpaper that dulls the shattered edges of the broken glass

the feelings stay salient

i associate moments with music
songs are a time machine
the feelings stay salient
no matter how long has passed

alicia keys and snow patrol
on the drive home from my grandma's house
those songs were the only way
my parents could get me to stop crying
from missing her so much

long live by taylor swift
my dad put it on before every soccer game
to hype me up
he knew what i lacked in talent
i made up for in morale

somewhere only we know
i'm performing in a singing showcase at a summer camp
despite my less than stellar vocals
the auditorium is dark and the chorus is loud
my grandma's hands in the air
lost in the music

post malone and tracy chapman
suddenly i'm fifteen years old in the car with my mom
driving home from cross country practice every autumn evening
venting about the amount of homework i had
laughing as she told stories about listening to music
with her college roommates
sharing songs from each of our generations

the dropkick murphys and the saw doctors
it's st. patrick's day weekend

my family's christmas
the sense of community and family
my dad and i are running up a hill in the race
my brother and i catching beads as a parade float zooms by
my mom puts shamrock tattoos on my cheeks
they were longer lasting than we realized

i can't smile without you and home
every time those songs come on
i know it's you sending a sign

dave matthews and coldplay
my parents are dancing in our dim kitchen
my mom pulls me out into our carpeted dance floor
i have two left feet but here i feel safe
here i feel free
we dance late into sunday night
it becomes a tradition
we're tired on monday but we never care

the first few notes of all too well
transport me back to november of senior year
my brother and i belting the lyrics
on long drives
we were both going through it
we couldn't relate to the song
but oh we thought we did

fine line and falling
my heart feels truly broken for the first time
alone in my car
i feel the lyrics injected into my bloodstream
they help me realize that feeling deeply isn't my weakness
it's a power i can harness

noah kahan comes on in the car

and my mom is driving me back and forth
from college
i think my life is at its lowest
she's busy but always makes time for the drive
the car is our reprieve from reality
we sing and laugh or cry
sometimes both
when i hear his music now all i want to do is hug my mom

kelsea ballerini
the first songs i listened to after a break up
one of my own doing
she made me feel seen
eased the the guilt i felt in the pit of my stomach
i made the hard choice
but i found myself

lorde and gracie abrams
my friends and i are sitting on the porch of our college house
laughing about a moment
we've been talking about for hours
getting ready to go out
the song that comes on the playlist first
we always skip it
changing our outfit seven times
making our own fun
eating bags of chips upon our return

i associate moments with music
lyrics and melodies are my time machine
the feelings stay salient
encapsulated in songs

too young to do the right thing

i'm too young to do the right thing
too young to be moral
regressing
growing down instead of growing up
i always felt an obligation
to be wise beyond my years
to make the right choice
to walk the tightrope of perfection
until it dawned on me
one thursday night
i'm too young to do the right thing
so i cut my hair
and changed my life
found my best friends
who would never steer me wrong
the friends i know will be here
for the rest of my life
we found a principle to live by
collecting stories for each other
saying yes
laughing through the let downs
and stupid mistakes
because at the end of the day
our spontaneity and imperfections
create the stories that bond us together
i said goodbye
to the perfectionist dictator in my head
and let the free spirit
out of her cage
i gave her permission to run wild
to mess up
to make the wrong choices
to pursue her wants
to be messy

to fall in love
to fall apart
to fall out of routine
to gather stories
to eat the cookie
and skip the workout
to drink too much
and talk too loud
and say too much
to stay out too late
when you have to get up too early
to follow the beat of her heart
even when she's unsure where it's headed
it was then i finally realized
that the chaotic, messy, and imperfect moments
are what makes life worth it
it's what gives you stories to pass down
it's what gives you depth
what gives you character
what gives you empathy
which is how i realized
that the best thing
i can do for myself
right now
is make the wrong choice

my brother and i

since i first got my license
my brother and i
would go on long drives
around our town
from sixteen to twenty one
from ten to fifteen
the growing pains of high school to college
the awkward wolf pit that is middle school
our lives have changed drastically
we've been on top of the word
and overwhelmingly sad
but no matter what
we get in the car
just the two of us
and drive
we don't always understand
what the other is going through
but with one look
we always know
what the other one needs
hey, do you want to go for a drive?
sometimes we vent
sometimes we sing at the top of our lungs
sometimes we sit in silence
sipping coke for him and diet coke for me
we have a niche array of songs
memories that only the two of us share
old miley cyrus and kesha
taylor swift and lauren spencer smith
something always gets us laughing
and on the days we're really struggling
a belly laugh in the car
is monumental
we have new problems

but we drive past the same houses
the one that's been in desperate need of a power wash
for five years
the ones we talk about living in
in the future
we share thoughts we don't tell anyone else
kept in a vault
that only siblings share
he thinks i drive for him
which is true
but his presence
helps me more
than he'll ever know
because somewhere
in those five years of driving
he stopped being my brother
and started being my best friend

flirt

you flirt
with the word
love
like it's a girl
you want to bring home
to your parents
slip it in casually
yet
boldly
grazing the surface
treading the fine line
between us
flirting with it
like a girl
you're scared to talk to
but can't get out of your head
so
go ahead
i'll keep listening
as you tell me
you love my smile
my eyes
my mind
as you say
i love everything about you
while i wonder
what it means

a new frontier

she spent her days searching for love
like a pioneer pushing towards a new frontier

the movies and books she read
made connection seem simple
made toxic seem beautiful
they did not prepare her for the rough terrain
that puzzled her no matter how many times
she trudged through it

the boys who left with no warning
the ones who promised to stay but performed the best
disappearing acts
the *do not enter* and *caution* signs
she ignored or thought she could remedy
the ones who should have been right but ignited nothing inside
her
the ones who took every last drop of water she had left

it wasn't until her face was void of color
her eyes bleak
and her limbs heavy
that she realized all the love she truly needed
must come from herself

in fact
the love she had for herself
would be the most powerful type of all
it was a shield and warm blanket
it was all the resources she would need to climb to the top
it was resilience and grace
it was compassion and acceptance

most of all

it was a type of love that would never betray her
that wasn't all she had though

the love of her mother who wiped every tear
even though she did not cause a single one of them

the love of her brother who was on her side
even when she was alarmingly wrong

the love of her father who had his quiet way
of easing her anxieties

the love of her black lab
who would lay his head on her when she came home

the irreplaceable love of her friends
who provided her with a sense of girlhood she never had before
the friends who would listen for hours
even when it was inevitably dramatic and repetitive
the strongest chosen family relationship she knew

she stopped pushing forward on that frontier
surrounded by all the love she'd ever need
but open to whatever came next
she settled and knew her heart was content
love would find her
the right type always did

my broken pieces

my brokenness
makes me creative
it's a way of turning pain
into words
into meaning
a way of healing
of putting my pieces
back together
while the dust settles
a way of making all of the bad
worth something invaluable
my broken pieces
aren't a weakness
but a weapon
one that nobody
can take from me

the problem with being 21

the problem with being 21 is that it's the first time in your life
where the path forward has not been chartered for you

you crave fun and freedom
late nights and shots of tequila
while simultaneously wanting to get your life together

you want to show yourself off to the world
but also curl into a ball and hide

you cling to the teenage years but beg for adulthood
stuck between past and present
cringing from the old version of you
but terrified to grow up

everyone tells you you're in your prime
you love that
except it also haunts you on the nights you can't sleep

you worry this is the best it may ever get

you're more confident than you've ever been
but insecurities fill your bones like marrow

reckless
but cautious
you love to disguise recklessness with caution
love to claim you're not diving in head first
when you're already drowning in the deep end of the pool

you crave the toxic passionate relationships
you see on tv and read in books
but still get surprised when it hurts like hell
love is more serious now

it cuts you up in ways your 18 year old self
couldn't have imagined

you're in a constant tug of war
between people pleasing
and the need to put yourself first
you're starting to learn that taking care of yourself isn't selfish
but haven't quite mastered the art

you search for meaning and long for a world devoid of screens
but you can't help but doom scroll every night
and put immense weight in how long it takes him to reply

because at 21
you're a walking contradiction
who can't figure out which side of you
is going to win the war

the contradictions are endless
on the bad days that makes you feel like a mess
on the good days you realize you are a duality

there's power in that

because here's the other problem with being 21
you're a mess most of the time
but everyone forgets to tell you that you're supposed to be

there's constant stress
you like to blame it on seasonal depression
or mercury being in retrograde
and ignore the underlying causes
but there's also constant fun
wild once in a lifetime nights
you'll never get back

your best friends are a road map in this phase of life
they wipe your tears
and smack you in the head when you need
you know in your gut when you've found your people

and at 21
you've finally grasped the temporary nature of life
you're learning that some people
are only meant to stay for a season or two
but it still hurts to watch them walk away

you're learning to believe in time's power to heal
to dull the edge of the sharp feelings
you thought you would never move on from
but you look back and smile
because you did

you're learning who you are
even when you don't know what you want

you understand now how fast time moves
you're constantly wishing for more of it
an extra hour, an extra day, just one more year
you're now one of those people
you used to roll your eyes at when they said
it goes by so fast

and that's the problem with being 21
it really does

conversations in parked cars

i was wrong before
a lot of good
can
come
from
conversations
in
parked cars

www.ingramcontent.com/pod-product-compliance
Lightning Source LLC
LaVergne TN
LVHW052022080426
835513LV00018B/2117